TO THE

CENTER OF THE

EARTH

TO THE
CENTER OF THE
EARTH

MICHAEL
FRIED

[*Farrar, Straus and Giroux, New York*]

Library of Congress Cataloging-in-Publication Data
Fried, Michael.
To the center of the earth : poems / Michael Fried. — 1st ed.
p.   cm.
I. Title.
PS3556.R48825 T6   1994   811'.54—dc20   94-7552   CIP

ACKNOWLEDGMENTS
Some of the poems in this book have appeared in two pamphlets,
Other Hands (Oxford, England: Fantasy Press, 1962) and
Appetites (Oxford: The Review, 1964); in a volume entitled
Powers (London: The Review, 1973); and in the following
journals in this country and in England: Agni, American Poetry
Review, Antioch Review, Paris Review, Partisan Review,
Princeton Alumni Weekly, The Review, The Times Literary
Supplement, and Western Humanities Review.

Title page art: Mazeppa, by Géricault
Courtesy of Yale University Art Gallery
Gift of Charles Y. Lazarus, B.A., 1936

To R.

The flash of lightning seen through closed eyelids

Contents

[III] Powers

[IV] The Flash of Lightning

[V] To the Center of the Earth

[I]

OTHER HANDS

Other Hands

My hands on your body encountering other hands
Take sanctuary in fistfuls of your thick hair.
You stare because it hurts and my hands drop.
This dumbness after pain is our true element.

And now it's my skin moving under your hands,
And my lips opening between your bitter teeth,
And mine the awkward tense features softening
In the uncertain focus of your gaze.

The Answer

Loving as I do the nauseous moment
Before the green wave destroys itself,
When it is held upright only by my
Imploring glance through to its brown viscera,

How could I fail to answer
The same annihilating clarity in you,
Once having glimpsed behind your green irises
Something brown and vast heaving over?

The Cry

Like a burning planet
Using up my air
Your face swings close to mine.
Like a glass of wine
That breaks against my teeth
Your hands make me cry out.
The anguished shouts of the elect must startle heaven.

Your Name

That passionate monosyllable your name,
Like some wounded animal's all but inarticulate
Cry, when the familiar hurt returns, on dragging legs,
After an interlude of sleep or natural anesthesia,
Spoken over and over by my own lips, wakes me.

Your Voice

Faintly ringing like the moist rim of fine glassware
Rubbed round and round by appreciative fingers
Before the perfect shape fills up with wine
And grasping fingers spill everything
Your voice bleeds into my sleep.

Packing Up

Your smell still on me, I delay washing.
Exhausted from having spent
Half the night trying to extort
Commitment from you where none is possible
I stack another room of books
Inside three tea-chests and nail them shut.
I wish words mattered less to me.

[11]

THE THUNDER
ORCHARD

Inside the Trap

"I am the right foreleg of a great wolf
Caught in one of God's traps and gnawed off
Through most of an otherwise mild night.
The rest of him still goes
On three legs through the game preserves
Of heaven, making up with guile
What he lacks now in natural gifts.
But the piece of meat that fell
Onto the bloody snow inside the trap—
What cunning could help me to forget
The rocking motion of my wolf's body
As I ran, cradled in speed and hunger,
Across the sleeping fields
Or the hot hare dying without a wound
Between my long jaws?"

Lines for R. P. Blackmur

July, 1959. Almost six years
Ago. Your throat sunburned, your white shirt
Dripping sweat, your entire gross
Delicate body concentrated in purpose:
To exterminate a black beetle eating a rose.
Bemused, dubious, but unforgiving,
You watched him work his legs until the death-throes
Were done. Later we sat enbalmed
In the clear gin we had been drinking
All evening. I kept trying to steer
Your demon monologue towards poetry
But, implacable, you went on talking
About Maine and all you had had there—
A larger garden, more books, youth, the sea,
And fabled Helen. Later still,
Having decided that I ought to eat
And having opened a cold can of vichyssoise,
You went out—smiling and apologetic,
Equipped with a long flashlight—into the garden
To look for parsley.

A Visit to David Smith

The granite hill inside the hill of pine.
"Listen. Do you want to know why I like nature—
The mountains and the birds and all that?
Because they're already made. I don't have to make them."
The rose light branching in the thunder orchard.

White Flowers

To the Memory of Seymour Shifrin

Your rare spasms of exuberance
Are fragile as this cold dusk
Through which we walk without speaking
Without feeling the cold.

Like the nameless white flowers
Your warm breath creates out of nothing
But insane anguish
They can be cut but not held.

Grandma Becky

When I called home from Princeton
And she answered the phone, I hung up.
That meant my parents weren't in,
And she was too deaf to speak to.

Occasionally I tried.
"Grandma," I would shout, "this is Michael!"
And she, lost, would shout back
"Michael? Michael isn't here!"

Verandah

From the brick verandah of the infant care unit
We watch the mounting killer wind manhandle the trees
Until it seems we are on the deck of a tossing ship.
But the babies are asleep in their stationary carriages
And two doctors conversing cross the lawn on steady legs.

Pain

They told me you had lost all your hair
And then that it had grown back gray
But when I finally saw you
It was merely downy, like a young rabbit's.

Your eyes were red of course
And your fingers trembled as always
But you looked in robust health nonetheless.
Naturally when I said this you were offended

And lit up yet another high-tar cigarette
To crucify the already unbreathable atmosphere
In that infamous office hung with effigies of poets.
Now your latest communication

Reaches me via this week's *Times Literary Supplement*—
Your usual dozen perfect lines,
A dozen eyedropper drops of cloudless pain
Which taken internally would surely kill.

Examples

For the philosopher the child is a source of examples
But to the father she is his beautiful daughter
And he admires her courage and her steadfastness
In the face of pain, confusion, separation.
When he smiles his left eye closes in anger.

Last Words (to a Dying Cat)

All right, tough girl, if it's really, really time for you to go
We're powerless to stop you. Just be sure to find
Another couple like us who'll look after you until the
   happy day
When we arrive to join you. And remember, Cleo,
No matter how good to you they are,
You're our cat.

The Sentry

The sentry stands in the snow
Unable to see anything
His hands frozen to his rifle.

His lips are moving
Soundlessly it appears.
He will keep watch like this

Hours days years
Until he is relieved
Or the snow buries him.

The flakes fall and fall.
In an adjacent world
The andiron in the fire

Breaks in the intense heat.

[III]

POWERS

Assassination

Black now as frozen lakes
The tall buildings of New York
Make awkward mourners.

Heart

Your body seen from the feet sleeping
White with rose blemishes sweet to the tongue
Wakes and turning over takes me
Blind to its heart.

The Mississippi River

Driving through Wisconsin at dusk in a light rain
Having just seen the Mississippi River for the first time
We admire in silence the lost profiles of our beautiful
  friends
As they strain straight ahead or turn dreamily towards
  merging traffic.

Highway

Your eyes behind their intense sunglasses
Might be closed or open, I can't tell.

Your body bending like the wide highway
Onrushing endlessly is motionless.

Grape

Mocking me you laugh and I glimpse it
Glistening with saliva,
Turning
On its soft bed.

Air

Having bathed together in the same water
We enter the same cold air
One at a time. You go first—
White,
Boy-haired, your body
Burning without flame like smoke in sunlight.

If I Could Make Time Stop Here

If I could make time stop here I would—
At the rim of this fountain
By the edge of this grove
In this blue light.

I think I would even forgo
My eventual triumph
To stop time here.

Depths (1968)

Suddenly there is nothing that is not revealed by faces
   alone.
America, like a hounded shark, not knowing where to
   turn,
Makes for the depths
Taking us down.

Seeking Escape

Seeking escape we visit the jungle greenhouse at Kew
But a tall Negro with an eye injury gallops up
Holding a bright red handkerchief to his face.

Kanal

My fingers are cold but I go on smoking,
The hand in my pocket touches my passport . . .
I am lost, obviously, or I would not be here.

The Room Itself Was Nothing Much . . .

The room itself was nothing much but they took it,
Seeing at once the full-length mirror on the closet door.
Already her hair is drawn back ravishingly in her husband's
  grip.

Wartime

Shadows of leaves on a cement wall
Tremble in the shadow of a breeze.

Powers

Our bodies are the closed eyes of a single animal,
Our states of mind so extreme they are the same.
Like the arts, we lend each other new powers.

Poem

So heavily we could not stand up
Under it, but lay down together in the parched grass.

Offshore

The same sea that bears the steel ships supports you and me.

[IV]

THE FLASH OF
LIGHTNING

Valentine

The sightseeing boat backs slowly out of the harbor
Then reverses direction and blasts off across the lake.
The swans on the other hand appear preoccupied
As if waiting for a consummation that has been and gone.
Overhead, against a heaven of impenetrable blue,
A heart-shape at the mercy of a great wind soars ecstatically
For as long as it takes to decide which way to fall.

Homecoming

In the late afternoon
We take a short walk, not to tire me.

An oil-truck slums in the alley next to the supermarket,
The naked flagpole shines in the twilight's brief gleaming—

Your beauty deserves to live forever
If not in these lines then somewhere else.

From the Heights

I wish there were something—some further thing—
That I could do, or thanks that I could give,
Or words that came to mind that I could speak
Hopefully, from the heights of my misanthropy,
Outlasting the effects of your sleeping pill
Towards destinations that are in flames.

The Flash of Lightning

The flash of lightning seen through closed eyelids.
The thunder falling from peak to peak.
The dark stairs climbing the bright stairwell.

Someone Else

For a moment I thought it was you
Again, your calves and your voice,
Your tailored style, your hysteria
Still holding me responsible
Not just for the food but for your appetite.

Memories

I knew casually two or three of them,
Whom even then I hated. Hated because they were
     worthless
And because they had had you and I hadn't.

If their memories are anything like mine
They have you at their beck and call forever.

Anniversary

You noticed nothing?
But my heart was stabbing through my chest.

I appeared normal?
Like a madman gesticulating on a trapeze.

You remember my exact words?
I remember everything except what we said.

The Pool

Old age that comes
On a desperate errand
But forgets its purpose
Pauses at the verge

Of a magnificent pool.
In its translucent depths
Fish and the shadows of fish
Cruise blandly forth

Or else merely loll
On the bright-figured tiles
Of its priceless floor.
These too have forgotten

In that azure sea
How they came to be there,
And for what implacable purpose
They were so deliberately stockpiled.

The Dance

My father has been dead just over six months
But last night my mother dreamed that they were dancing.
"Ben was never actually a very good dancer,"
She says, astonished by her romantic unconscious,
"Yet in my dream he was indescribably graceful
And we glided across the floor in picture-perfect
  synchrony."
And I, who wouldn't have known where to look
Had I been there, have no difficulty visualizing
A handsome Jewish couple in their late twenties (younger
By an age than we are now) captivating an entire ballroom
As the band plays on. I am the outcome of that dance.

The Blue

Three of us were reclining on deck-chairs by the side of a pool: Elaine (spokesperson for the Body), my father (dead almost two years), and me (in swimming trunks and no shirt). I don't remember what we were discussing when out of the blue Elaine (on my right) asked my father (on my left), "How do you feel about his body?" (gesturing towards me). If my father was taken aback he gave no sign. Instead he replied, in a voice charged with emotion, as though this were the one question he had always privately hoped might some day be put to him, "I can't tell you how much I like it."

Missing Shoe

How can you have lost a shoe?
And a belt? But especially a shoe—
Where could it have gone?
We search together
Under the queen-sized bed in our bedroom,
Under the smaller bed in the "boudoir,"
In your study, in all the closets,
In the plant room we use mainly for storage,
And still nothing turns up.
(You even check your office.)
I think the cat took it
To wear as a hat to a fancy-dress ball
While we slept, and *she* lost it.

After Basho

Walking with Allen
Towards the close of a muggy day
We stop to admire
Two trees in one.

A sudden shower
Flushes the birds from the high branches.
Deep in your breast
A wound is dreaming.

[V]

TO THE

CENTER OF THE

EARTH

Testimony

"—Sometimes too
There are potted flowers
Of exceptional beauty,
And once I even saw growing

On a vast black barge conveying tires
A miraculous orange tree.
These things only I have brought back whole
From the land of dreams."

Géricault's Smile

Géricault painting *The Raft of the Medusa* (the spiritual center of French Romanticism; also its carnal heart) was a man possessed, in the grasp of warring emotions so powerful and evenly matched his muscular horseman's body began its premature descent towards dissolution under the strain.

He cut off all his hair and filled his studio with severed heads and limbs.

Another fact we know is that he required absolute silence. Jamar, his young assistant, tells us how he once accidentally made a slight noise and Géricault—balanced on a ladder, perhaps painting the black *naufragé* at the summit of striving bodies who tirelessly waves a scrap of colored cloth—turned and looked down at him with a quick, admonitory smile whose irresistible feminine attractiveness moved him like a revelation.

The Wild Irises

Dying of thirst,
I long to share the fate of the wild irises
Each raindrop must seem to whom the size of a boulder
Flung down to devastate them with what they need.

Nothing More (Rome, 1960)

By the rules of a language game
They had devised between them
In a moment of inspiration
Already receding with the speed of light
There was nothing more to say

So they said it and said it
With words and without words
Accompanied by urgent meaning stares
And by an absence of expression
That could have made an angel groan

Until the topic was exhausted
And it lay on the café table
Like a tiny pair of paper wings
No one would expect to see fly.
Then they got up and walked away.

Somewhere a Seed

Somewhere a seed falls to the ground
That will become a tree
That will some day be felled
From which thin shafts will be extracted
To be made into arrows
To be fitted with warheads
One of which, some day when you least expect it,
While a winter sun is shining
On a river of ice
And you feel farthest from self-pity,
Will pierce your shit-filled heart.

Simple Daylight

It's true—if there were life after death
In an underworld it would be simple daylight
I would miss most, would grieve for
Inconsolably, would braid into every poem,
Every lament, such as this one
For what was lost.

Japan

Tired and empty,
I occupy a winterized log cabin
In a clearing in a snowy wood
In a country that might be Japan.

Each morning I catechize myself
In the hope that there has been a change
Either from or into the new man
It appears I've partly become.

Lunch arrives in a wicker basket
That later will be taken away.
But when I rush to the window
The encircling snow lies undefiled.

Towards midnight I shall step outside
And expose my face to the stars
And weep, not merely from the cold.
May their beauty appease me.

My best moments are those
When, in default of inspiration,
My hand rests lightly on the wrist
Of the one who writes.

The Light of the Moon

When Cleo was dying
And we didn't yet know it
She spent several whole nights
On the porch roof, communing with the moon.
When we called to her to come in
She ignored us. She knew
What her soul craved—
One more night in the open
Breathing cool air that frisked her whiskers
Until towards dawn she fell asleep under a bough.
Soon, soon, she would need us
To sponge up her vomit,
To console her in her misery,
To give her her medicine and cry.
To hold her paw between our fingers
While something loathsome collected in her throat
And the sour smell of the toxins she couldn't pass reeked
    through her skin.
But for the moment all she wanted
Was the freedom of the roof.
Although Death had closed his hand around her kidneys
He hadn't yet begun to make a fist
And she had matter for reflection:
How much is enough?
Do humans have souls?
And *where* does the water go

When it swirls down a drain?
—Age-old problems to think about
By the light of the moon.

The Limits of Safety

I call you from Chicago, exactly at noon, on a beautiful
  sunny day;
In Baltimore, one hour later by the clock, you pick up
  the phone on the second ring.
You say you've been walking in the garden with the cats,
Trying (unsuccessfully) to teach them the limits of safety
So that Eddie (in particular) won't cast away his young
  life under the wheels of a car.
The trouble is he's an impetuous boy
(The best athlete pound for pound I've ever known
  personally)
Who loses it the instant he senses a bird or other
  seemingly defenseless small creature within fifty feet.
What hope is there for him? you ask. And for us his
  anxious guardians?
—Better, perhaps, simply to enjoy his headlong sprints
  and leaps and plunges,
His innocent tigerlike face with its expressionless smile
  and permanently startled eyes,
His independently mobile ears that seem as if attached
  by wires to the least flicker of sound,
And his gorgeous, lanolin-exuding white fur with orange
  markings that could have been designed by Braque.
(His best trick, a winner every time, is when he finds
  me reading
On the john and performs slow, affectionate somersaults
  over my shoes.)

Cloudburst

Once in my life
I experienced a true cloudburst.
That was outside Oxford
Walking in an open field.
Mist rolled towards me—
Actually it was a wave
That broke over my head
In an unending deluge
In which the world almost drowned.
Then just in time it stopped,
The mist rolled away,
I stood there drenched and shaking
Transformed into a bull.

Autumnal

Short flights heavily burdened
That take off like a dream
And, when they crash, burn through
To the center of the earth—

Odor

Your perfume, or odor—
All measure gone I remember it, my body
Remembers it, my body when dead will remember it
In its bones, and when after incineration
The bones themselves are pulverized and dispersed upon
    the air
As tiny motes of ash, they too will remember
(Dancing in sunlight, jostled by larger molecules)
Your odor without a name.

A Block of Ice

I stamp my foot and a black wave races across the field,
I close my eyes and white stones spring up that I must
 avoid,
My hand in the freezing water gropes for but fails to find
 a block of ice
On which to sign my name and the date and hour of my
 death.